Dear Parent:
Your child's love of reading starts here!

Every child learns to read in a different way and at his or her own speed. Some go back and forth between reading levels and read favorite books again and again. Others read through each level in order. You can help your young reader improve and become more confident by encouraging his or her own interests and abilities. From books your child reads with you to the first books he or she reads alone, there are I Can Read Books for every stage of reading:

SHARED READING
Basic language, word repetition, and whimsical illustrations, ideal for sharing with your emergent reader

BEGINNING READING
Short sentences, familiar words, and simple concepts for children eager to read on their own

READING WITH HELP
Engaging stories, longer sentences, and language play for developing readers

READING ALONE
Complex plots, challenging vocabulary, and high-interest topics for the independent reader

ADVANCED READING
Short paragraphs, chapters, and exciting themes for the perfect bridge to chapter books

I Can Read Books have introduced children to the joy of reading since 1957. Featuring award-winning authors and illustrators and a fabulous cast of beloved characters, I Can Read Books set the standard for beginning readers.

A lifetime of discovery begins with the magical words "I Can Read!"

Visit www.icanread.com for information
on enriching your child's reading experience.

To Emma
—D.G.

To Rosie and Cam
—J.P.

*The author gratefully acknowledges the editorial
contributions of Lori Houran.*

I Can Read Book® is a trademark of HarperCollins Publishers.

My Weird School: Teamwork Trouble. Text copyright © 2018 by Dan Gutman. Illustrations copyright © 2018 by Jim Paillot.
All rights reserved. Manufactured in the United States of America by LSC Communications. No part of this book may be used
or reproduced in any manner whatsoever without written permission except in the case of brief quotations embodied in critical
articles and reviews. For information address HarperCollins Children's Books, a division of HarperCollins Publishers,
195 Broadway, New York, NY 10007.
www.icanread.com

ISBN 978-0-06-236749-5 (pbk. bdg.)—ISBN 978-0-06-236750-1 (hardcover)

17 18 19 20 21   LSCC   10 9 8 7 6 5 4 3 2 1   ❖   First Edition

I Can Read!

READING WITH HELP 2

My WeiRd School

Teamwork Trouble

Dan Gutman
Pictures by Jim Paillot

HARPER
An Imprint of HarperCollinsPublishers

My name is Ryan and I love sports.
Baseball. Dodgeball. Basketball.
Anything with a ball!

I play on a football team
with A.J. and Andrea.
They argue about *everything*.
If Andrea says blue Sportzgulp
is better, A.J. says red.

"Quit yelling," I told A.J.

at our last game.

"I'm trying to ask you something.

Do you want to play

on another team with me?"

"What sport?" asked A.J. "Soccer?"

"Um, no," I said. "Curling."

A.J. started laughing.

He spit red Sportzgulp everywhere.

"*Curling?* Isn't that what

girls do to their hair?"

"It's a real sport," I said.

"It's in the Olympics."

"Big deal!" said A.J.

"So is trampoline, and everyone knows that's just bouncing."

"Fine," I said. "Hey, Andrea. Want to be on a curling team?"

"Yes! I LOVE curling!" said Andrea.

"I take lessons every week!"

"See?" A.J. said. "It *must* be lame!"

"It's cool enough for Mo Deen,"

I said. "He's our coach."

"*Mo Deen?*" A.J. whispered.
"The greatest athlete *ever*?
The only guy to play professional
baseball, basketball, *and* football?"

"Yup," I said.

"I WANT TO BE ON THE TEAM!"
A.J. yelled. "I love curling!
I love to . . . um . . . curl the ball!"

Andrea rolled her eyes.

"There's no *ball*. It's a *stone*.

You slide it on the ice at a target

while your teammates sweep a path

with special brooms."

"Really?" said A.J.

"That's even lamer than I thought.

I mean, even *cooler*!

Please put me on the team, Ryan!"

"Sorry," I said. "There are only four

spots, and Andrea got the last one."

It was true. I had already asked Michael.

And I *had* to ask Emily.

Her mom was giving us rides

to the rink.

Besides, A.J. and Andrea

would just fight all the time,

and it might hurt our chances.

I really wanted to win our first game.

If our team won, Mo Deen

promised to take us to his mansion!

I heard it's totally sports-themed.

The lawn is a baseball diamond!

The living room has a scoreboard!

There's a basketball hoop *toilet*!

I was DYING to go there.

(And go there, in the hoop toilet.)

The next day, Emily's mom
drove us to practice.

"Slide that stone!" called Mo Deen.

"Sweep! SWEEP!"

Andrea was good.

You could tell she took lessons.

Michael and I did okay, too,

even though Michael kept tripping.

That kid never ties his shoelaces.

I thought Emily would be annoying.
At school she's always running off
to the nurse, Mrs. Cooney.
But she wasn't a crybaby at all.
Even when the Zamboni ran into her.

"Great job, everybody!" said Mo.

He gave us all high fives.

High fives! From Mo Deen!

I felt kind of bad

that A.J. was missing it.

Two weeks later,

it was time for the big match.

The other team looked tough.

But so did we.

The stands filled up with fans.

I saw our teacher, Mr. Cooper.

And Mr. Klutz, the principal.

"There's Mrs. Cooney!" said Emily.

"Come on, team!" Mo called.

"It's curling time!"

Andrea slid the first stone.

Michael and Emily swept.

I stood behind the target

and yelled directions.

"Sweep left! Now right!"

The stone landed on the target!

Then we switched places.

We hit the target *again*.

And we *kept* on hitting it!

All we had to do was score

one more time to win!

"We've got this, guys!" I yelled.

Then . . . Michael tripped.

"OW!" he shouted. "My nose!"

Mrs. Cooney rushed over.

"It may be broken," she said.

"Now what do we do?" I cried.

"I'll play!" someone called.

It was A.J.!

"You don't know how," said Andrea.

A.J. grabbed a broom.

"Yes, I do. I watched you prac—

I mean, it's just so obvious!"

"Go for it!" said Mo Deen.

Could this really work?

A.J. and Andrea—*together?*

I slid the final stone.

"Sweep left!" Emily called.

A.J. started sweeping.

"*Left*, dumbhead!" yelled Andrea.

"This *is* left!" yelled A.J.

"Not YOUR left, EMILY'S left!"

"You're saying Emily has a
different left than me?" said A.J.
"How is that even possible?"
"Because she's *facing* you!"

I *knew* it. I knew they would fight.

Now we were going to lose!

I'd NEVER get to see Mo's mansion!

Then I heard Emily's voice.

"Guys, the stone is on the target!"

Wait—WHAT? We won?

WE *WON*!

Mo's mansion was *amazing*.

We drank from a fountain

that sprayed Mo's own

Sportzgulp flavor, Deen Green.

We ate baseball-shaped cupcakes.

We floated in a pool as big as

a football field.

And for the first time ever,

Andrea and A.J. agreed.

"You're pretty good for a girl,"

A.J. said.

"You're pretty good for a boy,"

Andrea said.

Will A.J. and Andrea

agree on even more stuff?

Will Michael start tying his shoes?

Will we all keep curling?

Maybe.

But it won't be easy!